ANGELS
on COMMAND

INVOKING THE STANDING ORDERS

ANGELS on COMMAND

DR. LARRY KEEFAUVER

Bridge-Logos

Gainesville, FL 32614 USA

Angels On Command

by Dr. Larry Keefauver
Copyright ©2004 by Bridge-Logos Publishers
All Rights Reserved

Library of Congress Catalog Card Number: Pending
International Standard Book Number: 0-88270-825-2

Published by:

Bridge-Logos

Gainesville, FL 32614 USA
bridgelogos.com

Acknowledgements

My deepest appreciation to Dave and Janie Hail
and the Alliance Group for their
encouragement and support in this project.

Special thanks to Sam Hinn, my pastor, and
The Gathering Place Worship Center congregation
as well as the YMCS Board and Partners.

Most of all,
My love and appreciation to Judi,
my wife, who patiently loves and advises
me on every step together.

DEDICATION

To the Ancient of Days who sits on the throne,

To the Son who ever makes intercession for us,

To the Spirit who indwells and empowers us,

*And to the angels who upon His standing
orders encamp all around us.*

TABLE OF CONTENTS

INTRODUCTION

For He shall give His angels charge over you,
To keep you in all your ways.
In their hands they shall bear you up,
Lest you dash your foot against a stone.
(Psalm 91:11-12)

I read this scripture and shared this book's initial teaching about angels on a Wednesday evening in our church, The Gathering Place Worship Center, in Lake Mary, Florida. That was also the first time a true story about angels happened as a result of this teaching. A young mother, Chris, listened intently to me as I described the way that God has commanded His angels on our behalf to protect, propel and prevent harm. She took careful notes. And she carefully wrote down this prayer at the end of the message:

> *"In the mighty name of Jesus, I invoke the standing orders of Almighty God to **protect** my family from every attack, to **propel** my family above every circumstance and crisis, and **to prevent any weapon formed against my family to prosper,** so that my family will not fall or fail but will be overcomers, more than conquerors through Christ Jesus. Amen"*

I instructed everyone present that when praying like this, they might substitute the name of any family member or friend for the word "family" to make the prayer personal and specific.

Chris left the service that night with her notes tucked carefully in her Bible. I didn't see her until the following Sunday morning before the worship service. As Judi, my wife, and I entered the building, she met us. Her face glowed with excitement. "I want you to meet someone," she said, leading us to a young woman seated in the sanctuary.

"This is Joan," she beamed. "I prayed that prayer you gave us on Wednesday night invoking God's standing orders to protect her." Joan's face was absolutely radiant.

"That's right," she responded. "I'm alive and here today thanks to Chris praying for me and God's angels protecting me from death."

Judi and I were thrilled as we listened to their story. After the Wednesday night service, Chris had returned home and noticed the light flashing on her telephone message machine. She listened to an alarming report. A friend had called to tell her that a mutual acquaintance, Joan, had taken an overdose of drugs and was in a nearby hospital hovering between life and death.

Chris did not know anyone from the family. So she called the hospital to try to persuade someone to give her an update on Joan. Finally, a nurse in the intensive care unit got on the phone and told Chris that Joan's condition was critical and she was allowed no visitors. That was it. Nothing else at that moment was left for Chris to do except *pray*. Of course, praying was the most important thing Chris could do. So, she prayed fervently for Joan. She prayed over and over again the prayer invoking God's standing orders for Joan so that His angels would protect her from death, propel her over this tragic situation, and prevent future attacks of the enemy against her. Chris prayed through the night, releasing God's angels on Joan's behalf.

When morning came, Chris made a decision to act in faith. She prayed for God to release His angels to prepare a way for her to see Joan and pray for her in person. She prayed all the way to the hospital.

Now, the intensive care unit is closed to visitors. Only family members are allowed to visit during specified times. No one else is permitted to enter. Knowing this, Chris prayed intensely as she stepped off the elevator on the intensive care unit floor. She asked God to send His angels ahead of her to prepare the way.

The ICU (Intensive Care Unit) was at the end of a long corridor. As she rounded the corner and the ICU doors—always shut— came into view, Chris was amazed. The ICU doors were standing wide open. She had visited other people in the ICU over the years and she had never seen the doors standing wide open.

"What's wrong?" she wondered. Chris cautiously approached the open ICU doors and peered in. No one was around. No one was there to stop her from entering. So enter she did and looked around the unit, immediately spying Joan, who was unconscious. She was lying in her bed hooked up to IVs and all kinds of monitoring equipment.

Chris walked immediately to Joan's bedside and was quickly flanked by an attending doctor and nurse. "They're going to make me leave," thought Joan. "But God's angels opened the doors for me to be here and I'm not leaving until I pray for Joan," Chris mused.

"Why are you here?" queried the doctor.

"To pray for Joan," firmly responded Chris.

"We will pray with you," replied the attending nurse and the doctor nodded.

Not only had God's angels opened the door, they had prevented any negative attack from the staff. Instead, Chris was now experiencing great favor propelling her over any obstacles and lifting her into God's presence for the purpose of intercession.

Chris took out her piece of paper with the prayer she had written down from my Wednesday night message on commanding angels. Taking Joan's hand, Chris prayed and both the nurse and doctor prayed with her. Amazing! Chris prayed for Joan to be protected from death and to recover fully.

Upon saying "Amen," Chris opened her eyes and gazed into Joan's face. Suddenly Joan stirred. Her eyes opened and she looked with shock and surprise at Chris. Quickly the doctor and nurse moved Chris out of the way and began to work with Joan. Within an hour she was off her respirator, and all the monitoring equipment was removed. She was sitting up in a chair next to her bed … completely well!

As Chris told this story to Judi and me there in the church, we were very excited. We asked Joan what she had experienced. Joan shared that her depression had been so great that she had taken an overdose of her medication, hoping to die. The next thing she remembered, she was looking into the face of Chris. But such a bright light was glowing from Chris' face that it wasn't Chris she saw.

"I was looking directly into an angel's face. The room was filled with angels!"

To this day, Joan's life has radically, radiantly changed. She is saved and filled with the joy of the Lord. She and Chris tell everyone they meet about God's grace in releasing angels for both of them in protecting, propelling and preventing harm.

The Genesis of This Message

So what prompted my interest in angels and studying the Scriptures to further understand how angels interface with believers in a real and practical way? It all started with a comment from a friend.

"You can command angels," declared my colleague in ministry. I shook my head in disbelief. Images of spiritual warfare and demonic versus angelic collisions clouded my brain. I tried to excuse myself quickly from this "flaky" encounter, but the unfamiliar tenor of his declaration stirred my interest. Surely such a claim was groundless, or was it?

Slowly, clarity began to sort out the questions posed by such an astounding claim. The questions that must be answered emerged:

- Who commands angels, and by what authority?
- How do angels respond, and what do they do?
- Am I, as a believer, in the chain of command for angels?
- If I have delegated authority to command angels, when should I act?
- And what spiritual blessings have I missed by failing to act?

Obviously, angels are created and commanded by the triune God. Throughout Scripture we read how God sends angels as messengers, as He did with Gabriel, and sends warrior angels like Michael, who are at war against principalities and powers of darkness. Elisha and his servant saw angels camped around their city poised to do battle on their behalf. Angels ministered to Jesus in the wilderness and opened prison doors for the apostle Peter.

So, what do angels do on my behalf? How can I understand their power and relationship to me?

This book is more than a Bible study. Volumes have been written about angels. But little exists to explore our relationship as believers to angels. And even less exists describing how they are commanded on our behalf to serve and protect us.

In the coming pages, I invite you to journey inside the descriptive reports of how angels operated throughout the Scripture. However, this is more than a historical reflection. What you are about to read will allow you to understand the possibilities set before you as a born-again child of the living God to personally invoke the standing Orders of God in commanding angels.

A close friend and colleague, Dr. Tom Gill, shared this true story with me:

"A friend of mine was planting a church in East St. Louis, one of the toughest places in the U.S. in which to minister. For more than a year, they labored. Before each service, his prayer team and he would gather for an hour to intercede for the service and the people.

"One night as they were in deep intercession and warfare, one of the team, an Assemblies of God pastor, had a vision. In this vision, he saw the principalities and powers that were in control of East St. Louis. Furthermore, above them, he saw the angels of God standing with their arms crossed, doing nothing. He cried out to them asking why they just stood by while the demonic forces seemingly did what they wanted to do. The angels replied that the prayer team had not called them into battle so their hands were tied.

"Immediately, the team began to call on the angels to come into the battle. Beginning that night, the church began to grow and mighty miracles began to happen as the Kingdom of God advanced."

This book is not about angel stories—an abundance of those books exist. However, the point of this story bears directly on the truths of this book. The angels did nothing because they had not been released by the saints to act. From the early church Fathers through the medieval monks into the Reformation and up until today, martyrs and everyday Christians alike have testified to ministering angels. Their existence cannot be disputed based on Scripture and on history. What we need to know is how to release God's angels and how to invoke His standing orders commanding angels. Throughout Scripture, God's people prayed and angels were released:

- **Abraham** *prayed* **and two angels** were loosed to go to Sodom and **save Lot's family** (Genesis chapters 18-19).

- Moses *prayed* and the Angel of the Lord stood between the army of Egypt and protected Israel (Exodus 14:19).
- Israel *prayed* and the Angel of the Lord appeared to Gideon to defeat their enemies (Judges 6:12).
- Manoah *prayed* and the Angel of the Lord came to declare deliverance coming through Samson (Judges 13:3).
- Elisha *prayed* and the fiery hosts of the Lord surrounded the city, protected him and his servant and blinded the Syrians (2 Kings 6:18).
- Hezekiah *prayed* and the Angel of the Lord killed 185,000 Assyrian enemy soldiers (2 Kings 19:35).
- Daniel *prayed* and archangel Michael overcame the prince of Persia (Daniel 10:13).
- Jesus *prayed* in the garden and an angel came to strengthen Him (Luke 22:43).
- Cornelius *prayed* and an angel appeared to him announcing the salvation of his household (Acts 10:3).
- The church *prayed* and the Angel of the Lord set Peter free from prison (Acts 12:9).
- John *prayed* and Jesus commanded him to write to the angel over each church in Asia Minor (Rev. 2:3).

You have been given authority! Through faith in Christ, you possess God-given authority to invoke God's commands for angels on your behalf, for your loved ones, your family and others for whom you pray.

No longer will you ever have to face the dark forces with a sense of helplessness and hopelessness. Your understanding of what you are reading right now will allow you to walk boldly in the authority of Christ to join hands with the angels He commands for you. Protection and spiritual victory have been appointed to you if you will simply exercise the authority delegated to you. Here's how.

Chapter 1

SEATED IN HEAVENLY REALMS

*And God raised us up with Christ and seated us
with Him in the heavenly realms in Christ Jesus,
in order that in the coming ages He might show the
incomparable riches of his grace, expressed in
His kindness to us in Christ Jesus.
(Ephesians 2:6-7 NIV)*

As a believer, you sit in heavenly realms with Christ Jesus. Jesus sits on the right hand of God. Placing your trust in Jesus, you live in Christ and Christ lives in you. Where Christ is, there you are also—in heavenly realms at the right hand of God!

You are in a place of authority.

You are in a position of command—in the chain of command.

Now, what is Jesus doing at the right hand of God? He makes intercession for you. Christ continually speaks to the Father on your behalf so that all of your needs are met. "My God shall supply all of your needs according to His riches in glory by Christ Jesus" (Philippians 4:19).

In ancient Semitic cultures, the right hand represented a position of high authority and power. That's where Jesus sits. That's where you are in Christ Jesus. And at the right hand of the Father, Jesus presents His petitions for you—your provision and protection.

> *"Therefore he (Jesus) is able to save completely those who come to God through him, because he (Jesus) always lives to intercede for them" (Hebrews 7:25 NIV).*

All of those saved have every need presented to the Father by the Son. Think of it. Your every need—physical, emotional, mental and spiritual—is being placed before God all of the time by the One with the authority to meet those needs. And how do many of those needs get met? By ministering angels. They are commanded by the Father and the Son to minister to you.

Imagine this. In Christ, you both hear and pray His prayer. Praying His prayer actually connects you directly to Him. No filters, no interconnect servers and no interpretations are required. Simply pray His prayer for your life as you act on His ability to fulfill His every promise as He fulfills the desires of your heart. As you begin to pray God's prayer you will see that what Jesus wants for you far exceeds your wildest dreams and imaginations!

> *"Now to Him who is able to do immeasurably more than all we ask or imagine, according to His power that is at work within us, to Him be glory in the church and in Christ Jesus throughout all generations, for ever and ever! Amen" (Ephesians 3:20-21 NIV).*

Become a participant in God's exciting plan for your life by praying what Jesus wants for you. His desires for you far exceed anything you could ever imagine. Jesus seeks abundance for you (John 10:10). And who does His bidding? Whom does Jesus command? And since you are in Christ, whom does Jesus command for you?

He Shall Command His Angels Concerning You!

Perhaps you have heard of guardian angels? Are they for real or simply figments of our wishful thoughts and imaginations? Remember the camp chorus, "All day, all night, angels watching over me, my Lord!" That chorus echoes the truth of God's Word. The Bible declares:

> For he [the LORD] will command his angels concerning you to guard you in all your ways; they will lift you up in their hands, so that you will not strike your foot against a stone. (Psalms 91:11-12 NIV)

Commanding angels involves simply asking them to **protect, propel and prevent** harm. Angels have already been commissioned and sent on our behalf to obey God's command, but we must act—not only to thwart our enemies, but also to resist our own temptations.

When a military commander issues ongoing orders for certain procedures, these orders are called *standing orders.* God has already issued standing orders to His armies of angels. Commanding angels involves you invoking the commands of God already in place on your behalf. The commands have been posted in the face of all your enemies. But if you don't invoke the commands—the standing orders, angels cannot help you. Help is available, but you must activate it. The power is there; you must turn it on. Having the standing orders of God in hand to **protect, propel** and **prevent** harm, the angels await your signal. What are you waiting for?

3

Confess this: *The LORD will command His angels concerning me to guard me in all my ways!*

Pray this: *Jesus, I agree with your intercession with the Father to command angels to protect me from temptation both without and within. Lead me not into temptation but deliver me from evil. Amen.*

These very words, when spoken from the heart of a believer, become the catalyst for God to release angels to **protect, propel** and **prevent** harm. Your willingness to address the Father in this way moves you from a spectator to a participant in God's plan for your life.

Protect. Picture the guardrails along a winding, narrow mountain road. They are placed along the sharp curves to keep an out-of-control vehicle from plummeting over the side of the cliff and into a crevice below. Hitting the guardrails may cause some damage, but life is saved and the errant course can be corrected.

Some of the greatest protection afforded by angels comes in the form of protecting you from yourself— your selfish wants and ways. Like invisible guardrails, angels can keep you from going over a precipice and into a valley of destruction and death. God's Word declares, *"The Angel of the LORD encamps all around those who fear Him, and he delivers them"* (Psalms 34:7).

Propel. Ever said to someone, "Well, under the circumstances, I feel lost and helpless?" You are not *under the circumstances.* According to Deuteronomy 28:13 you are the head and not the tail . . . on top and not on the bottom.

Some people seem to live from crisis to crisis. They are weighed down by every situation in life. Commanding angels means that these mighty, invisible beings are commissioned to lift you up and not tear you down. You live over your circumstances, not under them. You are lifted up and propelled into God's purposes and prosperity by angels.

Consider God's standing order for Abraham concerning God's angel.

> *The LORD God of heaven, who took me from my father's house and from the land of my family, and who spoke to me and swore to me, saying, "To your descendants I give this land," He will send His angel before you, and you shall take a wife for my son from there. (Genesis 24:7)*

Confess this: *The LORD will command His angels concerning me to lift me up in their hands.*

Pray this: *Jesus, I agree with your intercession with the Father concerning me to lift me up, cleanse me, and produce through me the fruit of your Spirit in every situation of life. Amen.*

God sent His angel ahead of Abraham to help propel him into the future for Abraham and his descendants. The land upon which your children set foot can be secured by God's angel. Are you ready for you and your descendants to be propelled by angels into God's destiny?

Prevent. Imagine sitting at a banquet table filled with healthy foods—whole grains, fruit, vegetables and fresh fish. All of these foods have substances that help your immune system fight disease and protect you from infirmity. But you must eat the foods for them to help your body's immune system prevent disease.

Confess this: *I confess that God has commanded His angels concerning me to prevent my foot from striking any stone that would cause me to stumble or fall.*

Pray this: *Jesus, I agree with your intercession with the Father concerning me, that the angels will battle alongside of me as I raise the shield of faith and quench the fiery darts of the evil one. Amen.*

God sends angels to protect you and prevent the enemy's weapons from striking you. His armies stand ready to encircle you. God promises that no weapon formed against you will prosper. The angelic armies await you to invoke God's standing orders to form a protective, supernatural defense for you, shielding you from the incoming fiery arrows of offense, gossip, accusation, condemnation and ridicule.

When you allow the Holy Spirit to make intercession through you, you cease praying your prayer and begin praying His prayer—the very prayer of Jesus to the Father (Romans 8:26-27, Hebrews 7:25). In the Spirit, you are praying the exact will of the Father for you and thus commanding the angels according to the will, purpose and authority of God.

You command angels not according to your will and wants but according to His will. And God's will is to guard, protect, defend and fight for you every step of your way. When you are about to stumble, angels lift you up in their hands. When danger lurks in your way, guardian angels encamp round about you to protect you. But you must pray. You must release them. You must act!

Too often, we fail to avail ourselves of the intercession of the Son to the Father through the power of the Holy Spirit. We rush into battle alone without warring angels before and behind us. Imagine earthly armies trying to attack an enemy without orders and commands being communicated by those in authority. Chaos and ultimate defeat would result.

Too often, we find ourselves wounded, embattled, and even defeated. Why? We have failed to pray His prayer commanding angels concerning our families, our finances, our relationships, our children, our work and our ministries.

Remember this. The angels are subject to the Son who sits on the right hand of God (Hebrews 1:3-7). In Christ, we are seated with Him on the right hand of God. From that seat of authority, we command angels who are called "his ministers a flame of fire (Hebrews 1:7 NASU). These ministering angels, empowered by the fiery Spirit of God, consume the enemies that we face and reduce to ashes any opposition to God's will for He is a *consuming fire!* (Hebrews 12:29)

Here's the chain of command. Seated at the right hand of God, we hear and begin by the Spirit to pray the intercession of the Son to the Father (Hebrews 7:25). Jesus promises that whatever we ask in His name—His power, Spirit and authority, that will He do (John 14:12-14). The angels whom God has appointed to us, hear whatever commands the Spirit prays through us and immediately implement those commands. That's *commanding* angels!

Be certain that you are in the chain of command. Just as you must enlist to be a part of our nation's military, you must also enlist to be a part of God's mighty army and become a soldier of the Lord (2 Timothy 2:3-4). How do you enlist? Simply by confessing faith in Jesus Christ as your personal Lord and Savior. Jesus said, *"Therefore whoever confesses Me* before men, him I will also confess before My Father who *is in heaven"* (Matthew 10:32-33).

If you have never done that, stop right now. Confess Jesus as your Lord and Savior, praying out loud:

> *"Jesus, thank you for dying for my sins. I repent*
> *and turn away from my sins and turn to you as my*

Lord and my Savior. I confess that you are the Son of the Living God. Amen."

Now, join me for a journey through Scripture as you experience angels as mighty men and women of God experienced them. Step outside of your time and into ancient biblical scenes as we imagine what it must have felt like to experience angelic encounters.

Learn about commanding angels as you relive biblical narratives in **solving** today's problems, **overcoming** today's challenges, and **winning** today's battles!

Seven Standing Orders God Commands Angels Concerning You

1. To direct you into God's plans for you.

2. To give you a special message from God.

3. To bring you confidence and hope when you need it most.

4. To protect you in a dangerous situation so fear is overcome.

5. To comfort you when surrounded by troubles.

6. To help sustain and facilitate your dream or vision.

7. To work a miracle.

Chapter 2

COMMANDING FEAR TO LEAVE AND FAVOR TO COME!

Angels may come with unexpected, unsettling, and unusual news. Take the young maid, Miriam (Mary), for instance. This teenage virgin heard from the archangel Gabriel that she would conceive a child through the power of the Holy Spirit. That child would be Yeshua (Jesus), the Savior of the world!

Now compared to that message, any message you or I might receive from an angel would pale in significance. But nonetheless, any heavenly messenger appearing on our doorstep would undoubtedly startle and surprise us. God in Christ is the same yesterday, today and tomorrow. The same God who sent Gabriel to Miriam and Joseph sends angels today as messengers of His good news.

Right now you may find yourself despondent, depressed, or disillusioned. You need a message from the lips of the Son prayed to the Father on your behalf. You need to pray His prayer for you. What is it? Simply this: FEAR NOT!

God has sent you an angelic message. Such good news could well sound like the good news of old, *Peace on earth to all whom God favors* (Luke 2:14b NLT).

11

The angels are proclaiming to you the favor of God. He loved you enough to send His only Son to die for your sins. You are forgiven. Your past does not determine your future—God does. . . . *His plans for* you are good not for disaster, to give you a future and a hope (Jeremiah 29:11).

God's good news proclaimed by angels long ago is now for you. Listen. Be comforted. You have nothing to fear! God will never leave or forsake you.

Meet the Angel Gabriel

Gabriel, one of the prominent angels in Jewish and early Christian literature, appears in Scripture in Daniel 8:15-27 and Luke 1:11-20, 26-38. "Gabriel" is from the Sumerian root word *Gabri* meaning *governor*. It may also mean *God is powerful* or *God's hero*. Gabriel may be the governor of Eden and ruler of the Cherubim. John Milton called Gabriel an archangel. Many authors and artists believed Gabriel to be a female angel seated on the left hand of God. The truth is that Gabriel is a mighty male figure who appears as a messenger from God and an interpreter for the people to whom Gabriel appears.

A Vision of Angels

There were seraphim, cherubim, and ophannim,
Who do not sleep.
They guard the throne of his glory.
I saw angels beyond count,
a thousand thousand, ten thousand times ten thousand,
circling that house.
Michael and Gabriel and Phanuel,
and holy angels who are above the heavens,
go in and out of that house.
They go out—
Michael, Gabriel, Raphael and Phanuel,

and holy angels beyond count.
With them the Head of Day,
his head white and pure as wool,
his raiment indescribable.
I fell on my face
and my whole body surrendered to calm
and my spirit was transfigured.
I cried out with a loud voice,
with the soul of power,
and blessed and gloried and extolled.
—*Two Visions of Enoch*

An Angelic Visitor in the Night

Let's journey back in history and become unseen visitors in a first century Hebrew home in Nazareth. The scene might look like this.

Another sleepless night of tormenting shame shook Miriam as she tossed and turned restlessly in bed. Back and forth, up and down, hands on head, feet on the ground, pacing back and forth, and crying now tearless sobs, Miriam's thoughts swirled in her head and paralyzed her with fear of the future.

The pale white streaks of moonlight streaming in from the window and dancing on her wall gave her wandering mind something to concentrate on while she tossed to and fro atop her bed. The thrill of her betrothal just a week before had provided meaning for her sheltered, innocent life. And everyone she knew had had a part in planning her wedding. But now that excitement had melted away into apprehension and worry as she pondered her uncertain future. Betrothal and pregnancy were not supposed to be in the same capsule of time.

Miriam turned over again and gazed at the moonlight's flickering pattern on the wall and moaned silently to herself. Every one of her girlfriends' weddings had been so wonderful. The parties and festivals were so full of promise and hope. It seemed that some of those wedding parties had lasted forever. But such a celebration was lost forever for Miriam now. How could she stand before the rabbi and her family much less her friends being six months pregnant? How could she look anyone in the eye. . . especially her beloved Joseph?

What in the world will I do? she whimpered. *How will I tell them? What will I tell them? Oh, Lord God of Abraham, Isaac, and Jacob. What will I tell Joseph? He won't understand; neither will his parents or my parents for that matter.*

Remembering her cousin Elizabeth's wedding simply made things worse. Miriam had only been five at the time, but Elizabeth's wedding deposited a dream in Miriam's heart for her own future wedding and life's mate. Memories of excited speculations of her uncle's "secret" housing preparations and the whirlwind of that week-long wedding party were once wonderful memories. But now they haunted her mind as only precursors of what might have been ... but now never would be.

Most troubling of all was the unforgettable portrait of pure virginity portrayed at every wedding she had attended that was symbolized by the ceremonial blood spilled on the pure, white sheet—but none of that would be Miriam's now.

Her lifelong dreams of honor and marriage had been shattered. Her family's name was now mired in the mud of shame. *I must remove myself from the picture,* she thought. *Why wait to be stoned? Why not end it all now,* Miriam contemplated.

After all, it would be best for all if I wasn't alive. Then others could start anew with my embarrassing memory buried. Others could get on with their lives and dreams, especially poor Joseph.

Joseph worked in his family's construction and carpentry business. He was a very trusting and trusted man. Yes, she realized that everyone would need some time to get over her tragic death, especially her betrothed. But in the end, Joseph and the whole town would be much better off. She would do it somehow, and her pain would end. But for now, in the strange, dark comfort of deciding to take her life, she would get some sleep and then finish things tomorrow.

Miriam drifted off. Then a burning light exploded inside of her slumber and spilled into the room.

"Miriam," said the ten-foot, glistening being, iridescent in splendor and glory, with a deep, booming voice.

"Yes, umm, uh . . . what?" she responded.

"Be comforted, O highly favored one. God will take care of you and will dispel all your worries and fears."

Then the angelic man flashed out of her presence and the room fell dark again. But this time the shadows that had filled her thoughts were gone—replaced by a heavenly glow of peace. In fact, Miriam felt that she too was aglow, shining with the glory of a new life forming within her. She repeated in her mind over and over again the comforting words of the angel.

Yes! She was highly favored. Yes! God would take care of her. Yes! She would marry Joseph, and the name of her newborn child would be Yeshua.

What others thought in Nazareth couldn't be controlled, but God has sent His angel—so He was in control. And Miriam—the virgin—could rest once again in God's magnificent plan. Somehow, God would make Joseph understand the miracle that was forming within her!

Suddenly the moonlight beaming through her dancing window curtains seemed to flood her bedroom with hope, and Miriam thought back to that day a week ago when the same angelic visitor, Gabriel, so he called himself, visited her room.

"Greetings, you who are highly favored! The Lord is with you," Gabriel had announced.

"Fear not, Mary," the angelic visitor had continued.

"You have found favor with God. You will be with child and give birth to a son. You will name him Yeshua, which means *God saves!* The Holy Spirit will come upon you, and the power of the Most High will overshadow you. So the Holy One will be called the Son of God."

Mary had trembled with both fear and excitement at the angel's words. She still trembled every time she recalled his words.

The Son of God! That's right. I will be the mother of God's Son. Surely Joseph will understand. He loves Adonai and he, too, is part of God's plan. Miriam softly spoke with renewed excitement and wonder.

In another bedroom across town, Joseph also lay awake. A nightmare had awakened him and sweat poured off him as he pondered his options. *Mary is* pregnant. She says it's God. I know it's not me. Could she have slept with another man? No, not Mary. She is too pure, innocent, and obedient to God. Yet, conceiving a child from God is too impossible and mysterious. What am I to do? Put her away? Let the rabbi and village elders stone her? Never! Run away with her and live in *shame forever?* A devastated Joseph swam in his fears, about to drown in despair. He sorrowfully remembered his harsh words to Miriam, his beloved.

"What do you mean, an angel, a ... a messenger from God pronounced you to be pregnant?" Joseph had angrily shouted at Miriam. "What sort of tale is this you bring me now that the whole countryside knows of our betrothal?"

"Joseph, please," Miriam had pleaded. "I know what you must be thinking, but God sent an angel and told me to ..."

"No!" Joseph cut in. "No angels! No God! Leave me alone!" Then the devout carpenter had rushed off in confused disarray.

Divorce, a quiet divorce was the only thing that could avoid public disgrace. Joseph sat up on the edge of his bed. Strangely, his curtains began to blow in a breath of air unlike any wind he had ever experienced before. *I will arrange to put Miriam away first thing in the morning,* he reasoned. Yet somehow, his reasoning seemed so wrong. And his mind struggled with the ancient holy words recorded by a prophet, *My ways are not your ways, saith the Lord.*

The soft glow of moonlight was mysteriously growing brighter. The wind moving through the room filled Joseph with awe. He, too, was about to encounter an angelic visitor, who would change Joseph's destiny forever! (Retold from Matthew 1.)

Commanding Angels: *Conquering Fear*

Regardless of who you are, you can know beyond a shadow of a doubt that when you are facing the toughest decisions of your life you are not alone. Whether you are facing divorce … abortion … suicide … running away … or simply the desire to give up, God has placed within you the authority to bring one to part the dark curtains of your despair, a messenger from God … an angel with a simple word of comfort.

God's Standing Orders for Angels
to protect you
rooted in the inspired words of Psalm 91 is:
"to guard you in all your ways."

The Angels Declare:
"Fear not."
(Read Matthew 1:20, Luke 1:30, Genesis 21:17)

Fear not! God is with you. Let God command the same hope for you as declared by the angel Gabriel. Hear the angels declare, "Fear not!" Encounter God's perfect love that casts out all your fear (1 John 4:18).

Commanding
Fear to Leave!

In the name of Jesus, I command the spirit of fear to leave and invite God's power, spirit and sound mind into my life. By faith I see God commanding His angels to encamp round about me, to protect me from every danger, and to thwart every attack against me. I command peace and favor to come and turmoil, tension, anxiety and disfavor to flee. In the mighty name of Jesus. Amen.

Chapter 3

COMMANDING INSECURITY TO LEAVE AND CONFIDENCE TO COME

God spoke of Gideon's future potential as though it were already reality. We must learn to see ourselves as God sees us and speak of His plans for our future in faith.
—Terry Law, *The Truth About Angels*

I n the book of Judges, Israel prayed and cried out to God for deliverance from the hands of their enemies. God desired to protect them and to prevent the weapons of their enemies from prospering against them. God commanded an angel to bring confidence and assurance to a leader named Gideon, who lacked both.

God uses nobodies. Why nobodies and not somebodies? Because somebodies are too busy, too important, too rushed, too stressed, and too exalted in their own eyes to hear and obey God. So take heart. If you feel like a nobody today, then this is your day for a miracle. The same encouraging word God sent by an angel to Gideon comes from heaven on angel's wings to you ... today!

In your weakness, God is strong. In your brokenness, the Spirit of God can pour through you as a healing ointment soothing the wounds of others. In your pain, God gives you understanding and empathy for the suffering of others.

Been abandoned? Then find someone lonely to befriend.

Been hurt? Then mend another's broken heart.

Been lost? Then help another find her or his way.

Played the fool? Now use your wisdom bought at a dear price to keep another from falling.

So you've lost everything? Now you are in a position to receive whatever God has for you. Those holding tightly to great possessions and past accomplishments rarely have the desire to let go and risk everything. But those impoverished in spirit, soul and body know that they have nothing to lose and everything to gain.

Hear God's voice today. Once you were nobody. That time was but a training ground for becoming somebody that God will use for His glory. Are you ready for the supernatural transformation from being a nobody to becoming a mighty warrior for God?

The Test

It's frightening when an overpowering army forages through its conquered lands, taking at will and by force whatever it fancies to supply its needs. Even more destructive is the cancer of hate and mistrust which vanquishes the conquered and provokes ruthlessness within the ranks of the conqueror. When that happens, terror turns disciplined armies into marauding bands, and peaceful people into refugees as sergeants are usurped by unconscionable foot soldiers and civilian populations become hunted prey. Such happened to the Israelites when they were devastated by their Canaanite enemies. War stripped them of dignity and reduced God's people to a shattered band of nobodies.

Dens and mountain strongholds provided safe havens for those healthy enough to escape when Israel was overrun by enemies not long after Joshua had led them into their promised land. Isn't it often the case that just when we settle in our promised land, even greater difficulties and tests come into our lives?

As numerous as a plague of locusts, Israel's enemies had entered into a pact to utterly destroy the unlawful inhabitants of Canaan who a half-century earlier had mysteriously conquered their ancestors' land. It was only a generation earlier that the rightful reign of their Canaanite king had been quickly destroyed by these murderous invaders. So now the conquered turned against the conquerors making slaves of their previous masters.

As the Hebrews had weakened from warring nomads fighting adversaries to sedentary farmers only fighting weeds and insects, the Canaanites left in the land seized the opportunity to rebel and kill the Israelites. Those who escaped sudden death were fortunate as the survivors found themselves being starved to death through the systematic pillaging and then torching of Israel's farm fields. Hunger racked the land for those who survived to endure its pain.

One such timid, beaten down nobody who attempted to hide out and survive was Gideon.

"Son! Where are you?"

"Father, please ... I'm down here again gathering wheat. I was able to glean last night from the remains of Lamech's field. Not so loud, I hear horses to the east."

"That's why I'm looking for you, boy. Midianites have been spotted heading toward town. Come, let us hide."

"Yes, of course! We must go! But what of this wheat, Father? I am only halfway through. And if they find it, we will go hungry this next week. Then what will we do?"

"Move quickly. You continue, and I will watch. Just pay attention to work. If I see them coming, I will throw a stone. That will be your signal. So hurry now and we will see," said the father.

"Yes, of course, you are right. Go watch now, and I will finish as soon as I can," said the young man as he nervously sifted the flax from the seed.

I will complete this in record time, and again we will *eat!* The young man encouraged himself as he fought back his terror-filled thoughts. He had seen too much death. Too many of his childhood friends and their families had been butchered.

Come now, hands, work quicker than ever. Come now, *hands* ...

"The LORD is with you, mighty warrior," said a booming voice that broke into the young man's nervous silence. Turning around, he saw a man ... a very large man sitting beneath his father's oak tree.

"Who are you, and from where do you come?" Gideon asked.

"Who I am is not important compared to what you will now do, because the LORD is with you."

But the young man struggled with the stranger's announcement. He felt that the stress and pressures of the day's fear and dilemma were playing tricks on his mind. And so far as he was concerned, God had abandoned both Israel and him.

So he argued, "But Sir, if the LORD is with us, why has all this happened to us? Where are all His wonders that our fathers told us about when they said, 'Did not the LORD bring us up out of Egypt?' The LORD has certainly abandoned us and put us into the hand of the Midianites."

But after he said this, the man changed shape in a wondrous transformation as he stood upright through the oak tree with a transparent body that passed right through the tree's branches, soaring high into the sky.

"Go in the strength you have and save Israel out of Midian's hand. Am I not sending you, Gideon?"

Although awed at the miraculous scene, Gideon still wasn't convinced. "What sort of creature are you that visits a no one such as I? I am nobody ... can't you see? How can I save Israel? My clan is the weakest in Manasseh, and I am the least in my family."

The magnificent being answered, "I will be with you, and you will see God strike down all the Midianites through your leadership."

But Gideon was still unconvinced. He was nobody. He was no leader. He ran from a fight. Mighty Warrior! Now that was a joke. So he asked the huge, glistening being for one last favor to see if he might wake up from this strange afternoon nap. He asked for a sign.

"Gideon!" shouted his father right then. "Something frightened the soldiers. I was watching from top of the silo. They have ridden away back toward the east. Something fearsome prompted them to flee in a gallop. It was the strangest thing I've ever seen. I'm going into town to get a closer look. I'll be back this evening before we lose the light!"

"Yes, Father!" Gideon replied. Then as he started to call his father over to share in his strange sight, the angel placed a huge glowing, transparent finger over his mouth, and shook his head discouragingly.

What manner of being ... what manner of creature is this that now looms over me? Gideon thought as a weighty presence began to force him to the ground.

Is this an angel? Is this God? His thoughts now exploded in awesome delight.

"I must bring you an offering!" Gideon acknowledged. "Please don't go away!"

"Very well," the creature said, and Gideon prepared a full meal for the "man."

"Place it on a rock, Gideon!" the angel commanded. So Gideon did. Then the heavenly creature, which now again looked like a normal-sized man, touched the food with the tip of the staff. And when he did, it made fire flare from the rock and totally engulf the meal Gideon had prepared. Then, as suddenly as he had appeared, the angel disappeared.

When Gideon realized that he had seen the Angel of the LORD, he shouted, "Ah, Sovereign LORD! I have seen the Angel of the Lord face to face!"

So Gideon offered another sacrifice to God according to the tradition of his fathers. The LORD said, "Oh mighty man of valor, since I am with you, tearing down your father's pagan idol that pollutes the town market place will be an easy task for you. Do it!" And Gideon did it, though he did it at night to avoid being seen by the people in his town. But, he did it, and it felt good. It felt powerful. And he did it just in time, because this angel appeared to Gideon for a purpose.

While Gideon was passing his test, the destroying armies of Midian and Amalek had joined forces to ravage Israel again. Huge death squads were forming on the plains of Jezreel. But the angel's appearance convinced this shy young man that God was with him. Yet even having seen an angel was not quite enough to convince Gideon that he was somebody important enough to lead Israel into battle. He asked for a sign—that God would make the dew of the morning appear off and on a goat fleece, and then he would be ready to be God's somebody for the task at hand.

The Spirit of God came on Gideon and Israel rallied to him. In fact, too many rallied to Him, because when God sends an angel to use men for His purpose, He only needs a few.

So twenty-two thousand men were quickly whittled down to ten thousand by first of all giving any who wanted the chance to leave. Then those who stayed alert while they kneeled to get a drink at a local stream were chosen for the battle while the others were dismissed. This cut the number down to three hundred. God gave wisdom to Gideon. He was transforming a nobody into a somebody.

Next God gave Gideon the wisdom to divide his three hundred into three groups of one hundred—and ensured that each was issued the weapon with which he would destroy this uncountable army that had been murdering and scattering the people. The weapons of Israel's army were a torch and an empty pitcher. And the last thing anyone remembered inside the Amalakite camp were these words that echoed all around them: "A sword for the LORD and for Gideon!"

The Midianite enemies were subdued before the Israelites and did not rise again. And the land enjoyed peace during Gideon's lifetime of forty years. (Retold from Judges 6-8.)

Command Insecurity to Flee! Invite Confidence to Come!

God sent an angel to tell a nobody that he was indeed somebody in God's sight. God does that. God uses those who are small in their own eyes to do great things. He takes nobodies, making them somebodies, so that when the battle is won, nobody gets the glory but God.

Gideon saw himself as weak and helpless. But the angel declared God's perspective of Gideon, "O mighty man of valor" (Judges 6). I challenge you to see yourself as God sees you. Simply let go of those insecurities which are keeping you from enjoying the fullness of His plan for your life. Turn your back on any lack of confidence as you move in His confidence.

God has commanded His angels to lift you up and propel you above any poor self-image or victim mentality that circumstances might have tried to imprint on your thinking. I challenge you to make a personal commitment right now— even as you are reading this page in this book. Let it be a line in the sand—a personal benchmark—a commitment to rise above your failures and let the angels set your feet on the solid ground of Jesus Christ, your rock and your refuge.

God's standing orders through angels to you are "Be Confident!" These orders direct you to gather every "nobody-thought" currently residing in your thinking and dispel it by allowing the Father to command His angels to become an army for you. They are helping you put on the armor of God (Ephesians 6:11). You never go into battle alone. Rest assured, the battle belongs to the LORD! Never quit! Don't run! Face that enemy who seeks to kill, destroy and steal from you. The enemy cannot touch what belongs to the LORD.

Rest secure under God's strong wings of comfort. Allow the angelic message of confidence to underpin your advance against the foe. Celebrate. The battle has already been won!

God's Standing Orders to Angels
to propel you is rooted in Psalm 91:12:
"They will lift you up in their hands."

The Angels Declare:
"The LORD is with you, you mighty man
[or woman] of valor" (Judges 6:12).

Commanding Confidence to Come!

In the name of Jesus,
I declare to men and angels that I am
a child of the Living God. As such,
I am royalty. I am somebody called to a
destiny in Christ to reign and rule.
With angels at my side, together we
march confidently into battle against
every attack against my dignity and
worth, and declare: "I can do all things
through Christ who strengthens me!"
Amen.

Chapter 4

COMMANDING GOOD NEWS, NOT BAD!

Angels of Proclamation
The special angels of proclamation have faithfully bridged
the centuries, carrying the message of God's will in times of
oppression, discouragement, and waning endurance.
God's restoring servants, His heavenly messengers, have
encouraged, sustained and lifted the spirits of many
flagging saints; and they have changed many hopeless
circumstances into bright prospects. Angels have ministered
the messages, "All is well," to satisfy fully the physical,
material, emotional, and spiritual needs of His people.
They could testify, "The Angel of the LORD came unto me."
—Billy Graham, *Angels*

When the angel Gabriel appeared to Zacharias, he brought good news. Amazingly, Zacharias simply couldn't believe it. So at the report of good news, he became speechless. The standing orders of God for His angels are to proclaim of His good plans for our lives. The heavenly hosts of angels announced the birth of Jesus. The armies of God want to declare to you and through you the good news of Jesus.

How often has God wanted to tell you good news and you simply wouldn't believe it? Are you more of a pessimist than an optimist? Do you expect the worse to happen and are surprised when good actually prevails? Has your faith been eroded by the world's skepticism and cynicism? Are you speechless in the face of good news and verbose in speaking evil?

God's standing orders to you and angels are for good not evil. God's word to you is good, not evil. Here is God's promise:

> *For I know the plans I have for you says the LORD. "They are plans for good and not for disaster, to give you a future and a hope. In those days when you pray, I will listen. If you look for me in earnest, you will find me when you seek me. I will be found by you. I will end your captivity and restore your fortunes (Jeremiah 29:11-14 NLT).*

Have you chosen to believe God's good news or are you still reacting to the world's bad news about your future? In your tongue is the power of life and death. You can declare the good news from the angels or you can destroy good news with a bad report, a negative word, or a hurtful phrase. Good or bad? It's on the tip of your tongue.

Speechless Before an Angel

"Praise be to the LORD!" shouted Zacharias, as the lot fell to him. "I am honored! I will honor Your Service! I will honor the Almighty with all my heart!"

Yes, it was an honor to be selected from among so many priests to offer the incense of prayer on the altar. Only the priests descended from Aaron could do it. And in Zacharias' day, there were many to choose from, but today, he was the chosen one. Zacharias would represent the people before the altar of incense in the temple!

Once the elders confirmed his selection, Zacharias rushed to the High Priest, who counseled him in the righteous ritual before entering the Holy Place on this most holy day of his entire life.

His "do's" and "don'ts" down, Zacharias solemnly walked up to relieve the priest on the steps of the altar. With downcast eyes of humility, the two priests exchanged places, and now Zacharias stood only a few feet from the holiest spot on earth. Then, with his special utensils, he scooped into his firepan the specially prepared incense from the well-stocked vessel beneath the north horn, and offered the first offering.

His heart raced with excitement. His face flushed with anticipation and awe. Zacharias overflowed with praise and joy. How many times had he offered prayers in the temple with his priestly division, and with his wife in his home? But those prayers paled in significance next to this glorious moment. Now he was standing where few were invited—where answers surely came. So he raised his arms and lifted his voice:

I thank you, O Most High, for selecting me, Your servant, to represent the people and bring honor to Your name! I praise you, God of Abraham, Isaac, and Jacob, for accepting this offering on behalf of Your people, Israel, and for honoring me to stand here today as one who loves Your ways.

"And LORD ..." Zacharias hesitated. He thought of the last words his wife, Elizabeth, had spoken to him. "When you are in the presence of the Most High, ask the Lord for a child."

Like countless couples before and after them, this devoted pair had longed for years to give birth to a child. Perhaps it is the dream of every married couple at some point in time to experience the most wondrous miracle any couple could imagine—a baby. Perhaps you, too, deeply desire a child and can identify with this couple's yearnings for a child. So Elizabeth had prodded, but Zacharias, as well, wanted a son so badly that his heart ached with longing.

Then mustering boldness never before felt, he prayed, "Thank you for blessing my wife Elizabeth with child. And thank you for delivering us from our oppressors and for sending your Messiah to deliver ..."

What had he said? Surely he didn't presume to tell God what he wanted. Trembling, he wished he could retract his words about the child. As he was trying to finish his sentence, an explosive flash filled the room with bright light. Suddenly, a towering, brilliant figure stood before him to the right of the altar.

"What ... what ... who are you ... what ... " the priest stuttered as he struggled to stay erect in shocked disbelief.

> *"Do not be afraid, Zacharias; your prayer has been heard.*
>
> *"Your wife Elizabeth will bear you a son, and you are to give him the name Yohanan. He will be a joy and delight to you, and many will rejoice because of his birth, for he will be great in the sight of the* LORD.
>
> *"He is never to take wine or other fermented drink, and he will be filled with the Holy Spirit even from birth. Many of the people of Israel will he bring back to the* LORD *their God.*
>
> *"And he will go on before the* LORD, *in the spirit and power of Elijah, to turn the hearts of the fathers to their children and the disobedient to the wisdom of the righteous—to make ready a people prepared for the* LORD."

Once Zacharias' eyes adjusted to the bright, radiant light, he could make out the messenger's figure as resembling a man. Then the light faded and he could clearly discern a radiant, white being who blazed with a fiery aura as bright as the noonday sun. With piercing eyes, he seemed to look right through Zacharias' white robe and into his heart.

"You ... you are an angel ... such as those which are written of in our Law ... and you have come to tell me that we will have a child? But how can I be sure of this? I am an old man and my wife is well along in years."

"I am Gabriel," the angel sternly answered. "I stand in the presence of God, and I have been sent to tell you this good news. But because you have not believed me, you will be speechless until the day of your child's birth. Never doubt the promise of the Almighty!"

Stunned and embarrassed, Zacaharias quickly sought the angel's forgiveness, but he couldn't talk. He struggled, trying to form words with vocal cords that would not respond. Then he helplessly fell forward, prostrate on his face before the altar, silently praying, *Mighty one of Israel, please forgive my unbelief. Be it done now as you have decreed. Teach me in my silence. Teach me Your ways.* In those minutes that seemed like hours, Zacharias lay in utter humility, searching his soul.

Oh no! The people! he remembered after a few moments. *They are waiting for me!* So he stood up and rushed out to greet those who were waiting for his blessing, but all he could do was gesture and try to explain with sign language the miraculous, angelic encounter he had just experienced.

Zacharias clutched his throat and shook his head to demonstrate his helpless lack of speech. Then he pointed to a cherubim fashioned on a wall of the temple, vainly trying to explain his angelic encounter.

"A vision!" shouted one worshiper. "You have seen a vision?"

"Yes!" Up and down nodded Zacharias' head.

"What? A vision of what?" shouted another man in response to Zacharias' head gesture.

So, again, he pointed to the cherubim fashioned on the east temple wall, and the crowd began murmuring, "Angel ... an angel. The priest has seen an angel!" Then Zacharias quickly disappeared back into the Holy Place before another question could be asked.

When his time of service was completed, he returned home.

Trying to explain his angelic encounter to Elizabeth was difficult at first, even with the use of his illustrations and writing, but Zacharias finally succeeded.

"An angel of God appeared to you to grant our request of a child? And you didn't believe him ... and that's why you can't talk?"

"YES!" Zacharias communicated with an emphatic nodding of his head.

At this, Elizabeth kneeled, and with uplifted hands, extolled the Lord: "Blessed be El Shaddai who makes the barren fruitful, then, my husband. So let it be done according to His messenger's word!"

When Elizabeth said this, a comforting presence overshadowed her and spread throughout the house. Within a month she was pregnant. So they decided to tell no one and keep Elizabeth secluded until the Lord gave further directions.

Zacharias' loss of speech was a daily reminder to the couple of God's promise and faithfulness. Once the presence of God's Spirit overshadowed their home, neither of them truly wondered at the penalty of Zacharias' unbelief. Being rendered speechless by an angel was a small price to pay for the good news received. They opened the scrolls and remembered how God changed Abram's name from "Exalted Father," to "Father of a Multitude" the final year before Isaac's birth.

For the first time they truly understood how speaking a name could release God to bless and His good work.

They studied and remembered how Joshua spoke and the sun stood still. And how the children of Israel were condemned to wander in the desert because of the unbelieving words of the spies. And how Elijah's words brought a drought on the land. And how Solomon's wisdom writings spoke so much of the power in the tongue.

But most amazingly, they studied and pondered how Zacharias' words were so important to God's miracle plan. Could his words have resisted the will of God Almighty? Every day Elizabeth grew just a little larger. She was showing now, but they stayed to themselves.

Five months passed. Then, one day, there was a knock and a voice from behind the door. "Elizabeth! Zacharias, it is me, Mary! Please open the door!"

It was Mary, Elizabeth's cousin from Nazareth. And when Elizabeth heard Mary's greeting, the baby leaped in her womb, and Elizabeth joyously proclaimed: "Blessed are you among women, and blessed is the child you will bear!"

Both women knew of the other woman's miracle. But neither of them fully knew the destiny their sons would share. So the Holy Spirit filled them and prophesied their good news.

"Blessed is she who has believed that what the LORD has said to her will be accomplished!" Elizabeth said.

Then Mary prophesied, "My soul glorifies the LORD and my spirit rejoices in God my Savior, for He has been mindful of the humble state of His servant. From now on all generations will call me blessed for the Mighty One has done great things for me—Holy is His name."

Still Zacharias remained silent.

Mary stayed with Zacharias and Elizabeth for about three months, and the topic of his silence was often discussed. They discussed how the same angel, Gabriel, had visited Mary not long after Zacharias. Unlike Zacharias, Mary had spoken the words of faith, not doubt.

What a wonderful time that was. When the day finally came for Elizabeth to give birth, her neighbors and relatives heard that the LORD had shown her great mercy, and they shared her joy. And, as was their custom on the day of the boy's circumcision, they decided to name him after his father, but his mother spoke up and said, "No! He is to be called Yohanan."

"There is no one among your relatives who has that name!" her relatives protested.

So they went to Zacharias, to find out what he would like to name the child. The suspense and tension rose as he asked for a writing tablet. Then to everyone's astonishment, Zacharias wrote, "His name is Yohanan." And when he wrote that, his mouth was immediately opened, his tongue was loosed, and he began to speak—praising God.

Then Zacharias, too, also prophesied in Luke 1:68:

Praise be to the LORD, the God of Israel, because He has come and has redeemed His people. He has raised up a horn of salvation for us in the house of His servant David salvation from our enemies and from the hand of all who hate us—to show mercy to our fathers and to remember His holy covenant, the oath he swore to our father Abraham!

Zacharias inscribed over the lintels of his doorway the wondrous words of Solomon from the sacred scrolls, "Death and life are in the power of the tongue, and those who love it will eat its fruit." And their son was a delight to them. Yohanan's (John) insight into his purpose was extraordinary from an early age. And they kept Gabriel's commanding rule: he drank no wine or other fermented drink. Years later this Yohanan, announced by Gabriel, would meet another one also proclaimed by an angel. His name was Yeshua. And this name, meaning *God's salvation*, would give speech to the speechless and reality to the good news announced by an angel. (Retold from Luke 1)

Proclaiming Life

As we have discovered, God's standing orders for you are Good News. As you continue to act on your faith in His ability to do as He says, experience the fullness of His promises.

Here's God's promise to you:

> *Because He has set His love upon Me,*
> *therefore I will deliver him;*
> *I will set him on high, because he has known*
> *My name.*
> *He shall call upon Me, and I will answer him;*
> *I will be with him in trouble;*
> *I will deliver him and honor him.*
> *With long life I will satisfy him,*
> *And show him My salvation.*
> *(Psalms 91:14-16, NKJV)*

God has commanded His angels to guard you; so rest assured in this good news:

- You will be delivered.
- You will be lifted up.
- You will receive God's answer when you call on Him.
- You will be honored.
- You will have long life.
- You will know the salvation of the LORD.

When Lucifer rebelled against God and was cast out of heaven with a third of the angels, those fallen angels, now called demons, continue to harass and attack people. But they cannot touch or harm the children of God who know their authority in Christ Jesus and who know the standing orders of God.

Fallen angels may try to distract and deceive you with bad news. But rest assured, God's plans for you are good. Declare the good news brought to you in the proclamation of angels. Refuse to poison the atmosphere around or within you with accusations, offense, gossip, anger, bitterness or backbiting. Speak life and the angels with you are mobilized. Speak death and the angels with you are paralyzed.

———————■■■———————

God's Standing Orders to Angels
concerning you are to propel you above
every negative word, curse or feeling.
Hear again the command rooted in Psalm 91:
"They will lift you up in their hands."

Hear the Angel Commanded to Declare to You:
"I bring you good news of great joy ... "
(Luke 2:10 NIV)

———————■■■———————

Commanding Good News

In Jesus' name,

I declare the good news of the angels.

*That all of God's plans for me
are good and not evil,*

*That I will prosper and walk in
God's favor and blessing.*

Amen.

41

Chapter 5

COMMANDING COMFORT

Angelic Service
An angel is a spiritual creature without a body
created by God for the service of
christendom and the church.
—Martin Luther, *Table Talk*

Stories abound about the visitation of angels, their protection, and comfort in times of crisis or death. Perhaps as a child, you were taught to sing the spiritual, *If I should die before I wake, angels watching over me.* God promises to order His angels to protect us whenever we go (Psalms 91:11).

God's standing orders to angels are to stay the watch, comfort and prevent despair, discouragement, **doubt and defeat.** Encourage yourself with these thoughts:

- Staring over the precipice of death ... angels watching over me.
- Facing the toughest decision of my life ... angels watching over me.
- Fearing failure or falling ... angels watching over me.

- Moving ahead into an unknown future ... angels watching over me.
- Trying to raise a family as a single parent ... angels watching over me.
- Looking at loneliness in the face ... angels watching over me.
- Moving ahead with risky surgery ... angels watching over me.
- Encountering a dreaded enemy ... angels watching over me.
- Battling a nightmarish fear ... angels watching over me.

You are so important to your heavenly Father, that God sent His Son to destroy the works of the devil—that fallen angel who seeks to steal, kill and destroy (1 John 3:8; John 10:10). You are loved, protected, and sheltered by your heavenly Father. He sends His angels to protect and keep you from harm.

Make the LORD your dwelling place. Run to the Most High as your refuge and place of safety. No evil can conquer you. No plague can afflict you (Psalms 91). *All day, all night, angels watching over me, my LORD.* His angels are watching over you and yours.

Archangel Michael Rebukes the Angel of Light

"Don't be afraid!" Moses shouted. "Stand firm and you will see the deliverance the Lord will bring you today. The Egyptians you see today you will never see again!"

Then Moses lifted his staff as the LORD had commanded and the massive body of water that blocked the people's way miraculously divided and stood upright. The waters condensed and thickened, and the sea bed dried to dirt, in a mind-boggling display of awesome might. Then the Israelites went through the sea on dry ground, with walls of water on their left and their right. Amazing!

When Pharaoh's armies pursued them into the midst of the miraculous highway, Moses lowered his staff causing the waters to return to their normal consistency, crashing down and destroying the greatest army in the world.

There had never been a man like Moses. And Israel knew it well. Sovereignly saved from the waters of the Nile to be raised by Pharaoh's daughter and taught by the best educators of his day, Moses, the prince turned nomadic shepherd, obeyed God's voice in a burning bush. Opposing the mightiest kingdom on earth, Moses lead God's people out of Egypt's bondage into Abraham's Promised Land.

Once the Hebrews were safely across the Red Sea, Moses led them to the mountain of God, Sinai, where he received God's Ten Commandments and the plans for Israel's tabernacle in the wilderness where the Hebrews could worship God.

Then Moses led God's people from Sinai to establish them in Abraham's Promised Land. A miraculous pillar of fire gave them heat and light in the evening, and a pillar of cloud kept them cool in the day. When the people had need of anything, God's miraculous power worked through Moses to bring water from the rock; food from heaven; and clothing that didn't wear out.

But there were evil influences working within Israel's camp, and the ultimate aim of the people's deliverance wouldn't be realized in Moses' lifetime. The people bickered and rebelled because the fallen angel, Satan, was also in their midst. Lucifer, or the "Shining One" Isaiah tells us, sought "to raise his throne to above the stars of God; to sit enthroned on the utmost heights ... (Isaiah 14:13). And for his foolish heavenly revolt, Jesus Himself said He saw "cast to the earth as lightning" (Luke 10:18).

So here he was, the adversary, stirring up rebellion within the hearts of the Hebrew children, and quite frankly, stopping their exodus party dead in its tracks.

Moses himself was forbidden from entering the Promised Land because of his angry response to the people's rebellion. After spending forty years in the desert with Israel's family, because of *their* unbelief, Moses was only granted a view of the land from the top of Mount Nebo. And once he looked upon it, Moses died and was buried in a secret location by God Himself.

Finally, Moses was gone. And no one in the camp was happy about his complete disappearance, especially Satan.

Why? Why would Satan dispute with the archangel Michael over Moses' body (Jude 9)?

Perhaps Satan knew full well of the people's love for Moses. And he was the master angel of light (2 Corinthians 11) tempting people to worship him instead of the God of Light. Though the angel of light in pride had traded light for darkness, he still knew about the commandments of God.

> *I. You shall have no other gods before me.*
> *II. You shall not make for yourself an idol in the form of anything in heaven above or on the earth beneath or in the waters below.*

Wanting man to rebel the way he had, Satan may have stirred the people up to find Moses' tomb and to make it an idolatrous shrine. God was the God of the living, not the dead. So if Satan could distract God's people from life with death, then perhaps their journey into the Promised Land could be thwarted.

Imagine this possible scene:

"Where is Moses' body? We want to pay him homage!" the people cried out in bitter dispute. Joshua could only tell them it was God's will that Moses was gone.

"Our great leader has gone on to be gathered unto our fathers, and God has seen fit in His wisdom to leave us only with his memory!" Joshua decreed from the foot of Mount Nebo.

Then Joshua pointed upward and shouted toward Nebo's peak, "God took Moses up there, to see the land that your rebellion forbid him to enter. Now he is with God, and you are with me! So onward now to the Promised Land. Our time of mourning is now complete. And our time of entry is near. So let us go forward, on toward the Jordan, where we will cross over if God is still willing to allow us!"

"Yes, Joshua!" agreed the people. Then they shouted his name repeatedly as a signal of their acceptance of him as Moses' replacement.

"Joshua ... Joshua ... Joshua ... Joshua ... Joshua ... Joshua ... Joshua ... Joshua."

Finally, Joshua was able to calm the crowd.

"Let us enter into God's blessing and future. Every place our feet touch will be ours. It's time to possess the land, for the LORD is with us!"

"Yes!" the people echoed! And the people relinquished their longings for Moses, agreeing with Joshua to go forward and move on.

But Satan would not give up. An argument raged in the heavenlies. If Satan could reveal the location of Moses' body, his tomb could become the greatest distraction and downfall for the people yet. Imagine the dead religious rituals that could be instituted: special prayers and holidays in Moab at the sight of Moses' tomb, special seasons of honor surrounding the dead hero, even new writings that Satan would ensure would be written as "holy writ."

So he sought Moses' body with other imps of his staff, but they were closely watched.

"Eeeaaahhhhhh!!!. . . Nisshhhhhh!!!!" Satan cried out into the spirit world. "The body of Moses will be a great test! Let me have it to prove you who are loyal to Elohim as fools!"

But his cries were greeted with silence.

"You weak mortals will worship this mortal of yours. Show me now where he is! I challenge you again!"

Then, suddenly, the night air erupted, catching fire in bright light, and Satan lay supine in the spirit plane with a fiery sword thrust through his neck, pinning him to the celestial floor.

"Michael!" he shrieked while squirming helplessly. "A curse on your head, fearful warrior. A curse on your god, you spineless fellow. If you had followed me, you would have been your own— and shared my rule. I would have seen to that! "

"Silence, you foul, fallen demon doomed to hell!" boomed the archangel's voice, shaking the stars. "I am sent to command you—doomed one, so hear me clear! Your search for God's chosen mortal is over!"

"But I ... I ha ... ha ... have been granted permission to tempt the mortals," Satan stuttered in an wispy, weak voice. "Sh ... sh ... surely your God is afraid of what will happen once I offer Moses' corpse as a foolish idol for the mortals' infatuation. The weaklings in the desert will perish if I am granted my tempter's request!"

"The LORD rebuke you, fallen prey! Return now to your petty deception and woes. I will see you again at the proper time. You will fall to my power again, worthless one!" commanded the archangel. Then the heavens fell silent as Michael disappeared.

Released from the blade of the archangel's sword, Satan turned his ear toward the camp of Israel again and heard Joshua commanding in the distance. *"God has said, 'Moses, my servant, is dead. Now then, you and all these people, get ready to cross the Jordan River into the land I am about to give to them—to the Israelites. I will give you every place where you set your foot, as I promised Moses!'"*

Then Lucifer took flight and discovered two Hebrews walking into the outskirts of Jericho. *The weak mortals are acting as one again now and are praying like Moses,* he thought. *What manner of attack can Elohim possibly bring against my stronghold here in Jericho? My deception is strong in this city.*

But as he pondered the approaching battle, Michael's voice boomed out again from above: "Kneel and watch, fallen one. Kneel and watch, foul fallen prey!"

Lucifer, fallen angel of light, was rebuked over and over again. The people who had followed Moses now marched victoriously through Canaan, taking back what the enemy had stolen and laying to waste the wiles of the devil. (Retold based on Jude 5-11.)

Lucifer: Fallen Angel of Light

The Devil acquired the name Lucifer when the early Christian theologians Tertullian and St. Augustine, identified him with the falling star from Isaiah. They made this association because the Devil was formerly a great archangel who rebelled against God and was tossed out of heaven.

The legend of the rebellion and expulsion of Lucifer, as formulated by Jewish and Christian writers, describes Lucifer as the chief in the hierarchy of heaven, and as preeminent among all created beings in beauty, power, and wisdom. To this "anointed cherub" was apparently allotted power and dominion over the earth; and even after his fall and exclusion from his old domain, he still seems to retain some of his power and ancient title to sovereignty.

According to the writings of the rabbis and church fathers, his sin was pride, which was an act of complete egotism and pure malice, in that he loved himself to the exclusion of all else and without the excuse of ignorance, error, passion, or weakness of will. Other versions hold that his audacity went so far as to attempt to seat himself on the Great Throne.

The name Lucifer was also applied to Satan by St. Jerome, writing in the fourth century, and other church fathers, in commenting on Luke 10:18: "I beheld Satan as lightning fall from heaven." The name Lucifer is applied by Milton to the demon of sinful pride in *Paradise Lost*. In Christopher Marlowe's play *Doctor Faustus* and in Dante's *The Divine Comedy*, Lucifer is the king of hell.

—Lewis and Oliver, eds., *Angels A to Z*

Commanding Angels to War

God's angels will war and defeat demons on your behalf. God's standing order is that no weapon formed against you can prosper. You will overcome. When putting on the full armor of God, don't forget the purpose of the armor—to equip you to pray. By prayer you release the angels to do the will of God: tearing down principalities and powers.

Yes, your battles are not against flesh and blood but rather are against every evil spirit that seeks to exalt itself against the living God. And your weapons are not carnal or in the flesh, but are spiritual. Rebuke distress and anxiety. Be comforted that the angels war on your behalf. Invoking God's standing orders of comfort and protection, the angels pull down principalities.

Consider this. Daniel prayed and Michael warred against the fallen angel, the prince of Persia. Michael was delayed, but not thwarted in answering Daniel's prayer (Daniel 10). So take comfort and be patient. Pray and release angels to pull down principalities and overcome strongholds in the name of Jesus. Pray and release angels in preventing any harm to befall you.

———■———

God's Standing Orders for Angels
concerning you is to prevent harm.
Psalm 91 declares:
"... lest you dash your foot against a stone."

God's angels are commanded to
encamp around about you and prevent
the enemy's attack from harming you.

Hear the Command of the Lord:
"The Angel of the Lord encamps all around those
who fear him, and delivers them."
(Psalms 34:7)

———■———

Commanding Comfort

In Jesus' name,

fearing the LORD in all my ways,

I declare the command of God for angels to encamp all around me,

to prevent any attack of the enemy from robbing me of comfort, help, health or security.

Jesus, comfort me with Your presence

and send Your angels to prevent worry, anxiety and stress from shattering my peace in You.

Amen.

Chapter 6

COMMANDING FREEDOM

Set Free
So, altho' I'm not an angel,
Yet I know that over there
I will join the blessed chorus
That the angels cannot share;
I will sing about my Savior,
Who upon dark Calvary
Freely pardoned my transgressions,
Died to set a sinner free.
—Johnson Oatman, Jr, and J. Sweney in the hymn
Holy, Holy Is What the Angels Sing

Nothing can keep you in prison! Prisons come in every form and imagination. You may be imprisoned by your past with its mistakes and failures. You may find that your present feelings or circumstances have you incarcerated and filled with paralysis. You may be in the jail of your future as you sit shackled by worry, fear and anxiety. God has left standing orders to set you free.

You are bound by guilt only if you chose to be. The forgiving love of God through Christ's death on the cross has set you free from sin and guilt. Accept it. Admit your sin, quit doing what's wrong and forget the past. You are free from the prison of inner bondages.

You are imprisoned by your feelings or circumstances only if you believe that freedom is impossible. The good news is that with God all things are possible. Jesus came to set the captives free (Luke 4:18) and that includes you! You are a prisoner to your present only if you chose to be. Jesus has promised to be with you and to meet your every need.

You are incarcerated by your future only if you chose to be. Once you trust Jesus Christ, your future is in God's hands, not the hands of your enemies, your creditors or your detractors. The cell door of your prison has been opened by God's angels. Why are you still sitting inside the prison of your own making?

Living without bondage means being set free from every physical, emotional, mental, and spiritual prison. No cell can detain you. No future event can dismay you, not even death. It, too, has been conquered. Listen to what the angel says, "Don't be afraid. I know you are looking for Jesus, who was crucified. He isn't here! He has been raised from the dead, just as he said would happen" (Matthew 28:5-6).

Bury your past, present and future shackles in the tomb, walk out the door, and live a new life of freedom in Christ.

God's standing orders in Psalm 91 include those to **propel** you out of your tomb, prison and bondage, and into the sweet air of freedom in God's Spirit. The hands of angels shall "lift you up" (Psalms 91:12). Invoke God's standing order of freedom right now! "You shall know the truth and the truth shall set you free" (John 8:31).

Freed By an Angel

The city was swirling with visitors and the air of expectancy that Passover always brought. The clatter of wagons, mules' feet, and oxen seemed continuous to Jerusalem's downtown residents for four days and nights. New vendors had sprouted along the crowded streets like perennials in spring. They lined the streets, selling everything from bread to clothes. The inns and home of every Jerusalem relative who could be prevailed upon were filled to capacity with worshipers from around the world.

But there was also an air of terror in Jerusalem this year. Wishing to win the confidence of certain powerful anti-Christian bigots, and more importantly to increase his favor with the Roman emperor Claudius, Herod Aggripa the First had been hunting and killing the so-called Christians of the Jewish sect known as the Way. Herodian spies had been infiltrating Christian meetings. Then after targeting selected leaders, Herod's death squads would pull them out of bed at night, never to be seen again.

Only the staunchest of Christian believers this Passover walked the streets of Jerusalem without fear. James, the son of Zebedee, used his public sermons and private conversations to remind even the most zealous Jews of Jesus Christ's prophetic decree to invite coming times of persecution as an opportunity to share their testimonies.

In James' last sermon given at a celebration of the Feast of Unleavened Bread, he reportedly shared Jesus' words of encouraging defense. Then that night, his family rousted close friends out of bed at four in the morning with the horrifying news that he had been dragged from his bed and led away in chains by ten hooded men. Four days later they heard even worse news—James had been beheaded by Agrippa. Not only that, but it pleased Jerusalem's bigoted Jews so much, that Agrippa was looking for the Christian sect's renowned leader Peter, to do the same to him. So no Christian group was safe in Jerusalem, and the search for Peter was on.

"Where will you go after tonight's meeting, Peter?" asked the host of the night's meeting.

"That's not important," Peter answered. "Our LORD told me how I would come home to meet Him someday. And if that day is tomorrow, even if I am to meet with James before the rising of the morning sun, I am ready to go. But none of that is important. What is important is the preaching of God's Word. So come, let us begin the evening," Peter concluded as the host opened the door and showed Peter into the meeting room.

The downstairs storage room of the Jerusalem business was packed to the walls with some two hundred people who had heard of this meeting. Some thirty others sprawled out into the basement's passageways lining the hallways and stairs.

As Peter walked through and over those crouched together in what appeared to be the gathering's front row, the cacophony of individual conversations, praises and prayers ceased. After moving behind a table, a beaming attendant unribboned and handed him a scroll.

Peter raised his arms, then led the group in prayer: "Our Father, who dwells in the heavens, we gather to praise Your name. We pray Your kingdom come among us now as we honor to do Your earthly will. Blessed be God who gives us bread to eat, and forgives our sins. We thank You for cleansing us from iniquity today. And we thank You for ... "

But Peter's prayer was suddenly cut short as four armed men sprang to their feet, and one uttered these words: "You! Peter of Capernaum are an enemy of the nation. King Agrippa has sent us as your invitation to dine in his dungeon tonight!"

The man then turned to the huddled believers and threatened, "Any who resists on this man's behalf will die tonight. These are the king's written orders. So if you want to meet your Jesus this eve, come taste the steel of these blades!"

"There is no need for that!" shouted Peter. "Take me now; I will go willingly. I will go. Let us be off!"

So the men surrounded and led Peter out through the city and up to a rusty palace gate. Passing through the walls and many guarded passageways, they finally arrived at a captain's desk.

"So this is the scum, eh? So this is the little Christ who has bothered our nation so horribly? Now, here, let me look at you," the captain mocked as he grabbed Peter's beard and raised his head. But he withdrew his hand quickly when a strange force from behind lifted his own head back, causing great pain.

Stunned, the captain let go of Peter and yelled into the prison corridor for his sergeant in charge. "Sergeant of the guard!" he bellowed at the top of his lungs.

"Coming, Sir!" echoed a voice amid the clanking of armor and rushing footsteps.

"Report to me now with the gate men on watch!" the Captain shouted.

"Yes, Sir! All men report!" rebounded the sergeant's voice now sounding with the footsteps of many men.

When the sergeant arrived, the captain, still stunned, but now very angry, commanded: "Lock this man up! Guard him closely at all hours. He is scheduled for execution at Agrippa's will. Chain him and watch him! If anything at all happens, it will be your head!"

"Yes, Sir!" answered the sergeant. Then he chained Peter's hands and feet and rushed him to a cell. He commanded the prison's four squads, forty soldiers in all, to stand by and watch.

"This man is tricky, a soothsayer or magician of sorts, the captain says. And he is an enemy of our nation. He is to be delivered to King Agrippa's good purpose, and if anyone here shirks in his duty of seeing that happen, death will be too good for him!" the sergeant bellowed at his second in charge.

The first night Peter preached and prayed until the sergeant had him gagged and chained between two men. Replacements were brought for the five who "fell under Peter's *spell*" showing their sorrow for their sin.

The next day the darkness of the prison made it seem much like the previous night. The soldiers not sleeping stood guard outside Peter's cell, while the two assigned to his wrist chains sat guarding inside.

Finally, Passover passed arduously, with no call from Agrippa, and no change of guard. Palace rumors filtering down said the next day would be Peter's last, and it encouraged the soldiers standing watch.

Peter convinced the sergeant to remove his gag after a relief break, and sat in silence prayerfully for the rest of the day, speaking only when questioned by the sergeant of his magic and devilish ways.

"The God of our LORD Jesus Christ has called me, He guides my will and ways," was all that Peter would answer, knowing more would only provoke him.

Then the word finally came down from the captain's office. In the morning Peter was to be delivered to Agrippa's courtroom. The same death squad provided by Caesar Augustus that beheaded James would be standing ready to execute the death sentence.

Night finally came, and the guard, now weary from broken sleep, struggled for comfort while fighting off sleep as Peter lay, bound and chained, sleeping peacefully between two soldiers.

Suddenly, a flash of light penetrated the dimly lit cell block and an angelic being appeared in the cell.

"Quick, get up!" said the huge creature while shaking Peter out of his sleep. As Peter came to, the chains fell from his wrists. The soldiers on guard were unconscious, face down on the ground. Whether they were sleeping or dead, Peter couldn't tell.

"Put on your clothes and sandals," the glowing being told him. And Peter did so. "Now, wrap your cloak around you and follow me."

So Peter obeyed and followed him—but he had no idea that what was happening was *really* occurring, thinking he was possibly having a vision like the one he received in Joppa a few months back.

The towering being seemed to walk right through solid objects as he led Peter through the prison's corridors. They walked by the first and second guards. Finally, they arrived at an iron gate which opened for them by itself, and they walked through it. Then they walked together, another minute, down the length of a street, and just as suddenly as the being appeared, it faded out of sight.

The lights and night sights of Jerusalem now appeared before Peter. As he looked over the city, he suddenly came to himself and muttered quietly, "Surely the LORD sent his angel and rescued me this day from Agrippa's plans and from everything that happened to James."

But then he wondered, "Why me? Why not James?"

When the full impact of what actually had happened finally dawned on him, Peter felt impressed to rush to the house of Mary, the mother of his good friend, Mark. When he arrived, he almost expected the outer gate of the house to open by itself. And he kept looking over his shoulder for further instructions from his angelic guide.

But neither of these things happened. So he knocked on the outer entrance, and a servant girl answered the door. When the girl recognized Peter's voice, she was so overjoyed, that she ran back without opening the door, shouting, "Everyone! It's Peter! Peter is at the door!"

Inside the house were many who were present at the basement meeting two nights earlier when Peter was arrested, and they had been fervently praying for him.

"You're out of your mind," they told the servant girl.

But when she kept insisting that it was so, they shouted, "It must be his angel!"

Peter heard their statement outside and thought, *It must be his angel? Which is easier to believe? That I am out here, or a heavenly angel? Have there been other angels visiting Passover this year?*

So Peter kept on knocking. When they finally opened the door, they were amazed. After warm hugs and greetings, Peter placed his finger over his lips, motioning for the group to be quiet. Then he described in great detail his angelic deliverance and told them to share what had happened with James of the Jerusalem church, before disappearing into the night.

The next morning, when Agrippa himself questioned the sergeant of the guard, the dazed soldier was a mass of quivering confusion, and could only think of blaming the sorcerer's magic on his troops' demise. After a thorough search could not produce Peter, the king ordered that the captain and all his men be executed by the very death squad Augustus assigned to Peter's death.

Then Agrippa fled to Caesarea for a while, fearing for his own life. And his fears proved true not many days later when an angel, maybe Peter's angel, struck Agrippa dead as he addressed a crowd of his own godless worshipers.

When this news reached Peter, laying low in Capernaum, he remembered the words Jesus spoke while ministering in the temple at Jerusalem: "For just as the Father raises the dead and gives them life, even so the Son gives life to whom he is pleased to give it."

Suddenly, Peter realized that hiding was not necessary. Agrippa was dead, but Jesus was alive! Walking Capernaum's streets with boldness and courage, Peter realized that he had really been freed by an angel from two prisons that miraculous night—the prison of Agrippa and the prison of fear! (Retold from Acts 12)

Angels Setting You Free!

What prison traps you right now? Is it from the past, present or future? Why are you just sitting there? Do something!

Release the angels according to the standing orders of God. The prayers of the Intercessor, Jesus the Christ, sitting at the right hand of the Father, have set you free! His blood has already been shed for all your sins. His death has broken any curse that would imprison you. His hope shatters any future prison that you might worry or fret about. So get up, get over it and get on with God's destiny for your life.

The Angel of the LORD has unlocked the door to your prison. It stands wide open. Walk out into God's presence and purpose for your life.

The Standing Order of God commanding angels is to propel you over any prison wall into freedom. Psalm 91 declares: "... in angels' hands they shall bear you up."

Release the angels to come and speak to you, "Arise, quickly." (Acts 12:7)

When you arise, the chains will fall off your hands just as they did Peter's hands. You will be delivered from prison just as Peter was!

Commanding Freedom

Declaring the standing orders of God,

I repent of any prison I have constructed,

I repent of any bondage I have accepted.

Through the forgiving blood of Jesus,

I know that God has commanded His angels to unlock my prison doors.

Therefore I command freedom in Christ Jesus in my every thought, feeling and decision.

In Jesus' name,

Amen.

Chapter 7

COMMANDING MINISTERING ANGELS FROM HEAVEN

Angelic Defense
The angels are the dispensers and administrators of the
Divine beneficence toward us; they regard our safety,
undertake our defense, direct our ways, and exercise a
constant solicitude that no evil befall us.
—John Calvin, *Institutes*, I, 1536

Angels exist to minister and to protect. An angel brought food to a hungry Elijah (1 Kings 17:6) and guarded little ones (Matthew 18:10). The promise of God is: "The Angel of the Lord encampeth round about those who fear him, and delivereth them" (Psalms 34:7).

In the old West, wagons would encircle a group of settlers under attack. In medieval times, the circling walls of a castle protected the indwelling inhabitants. In the Gulf War, tanks formed a protective shield around the infantry as war raged all around. So angels encircle us to protect us and provide for our needs.

Even as angels minister to our needs, so we are to minister to the needs of others. For example, "Don't forget to show hospitality to strangers, for some who have done this have entertained angels without realizing it" (Hebrews 13:2 NLT).

We can all learn some important lessons from angels. They announce good news, so should we. They minister to the needs of others, so can we. They protect and guard the weak and innocent, so must we. Angels are God's messengers, so are we.

But there are some things that angels can never do. They can never touch, hug or kiss. They will never experience the grace of God's forgiveness or the cleansing of Jesus' shed blood. And they will never be the temples of His Spirit. Only you can. Never expect angels to minister what only you can minister. In fact, the only angel God has for feeding the poor, clothing the naked, visiting the sick, lonely and imprisoned is you. Will you do whatever He commands you today just as the angels obey God's every command?

In order to release angels to obey God's standing orders, you must be in the chain of command. You must be surrendered totally to Jesus Christ as LORD and Savior. Have you ever climbed the stairway to heaven?

Stairway to Heaven

"Dumb mule, I know this is a steep one, but we are nearly through for the day," Jacob said as he led his animal out of a ravine. "To Padan-Aram! To good Uncle Laban's to find a wife. Carry me to my new wife. Soon we will rest. The sun is heading for earth's borders," Jacob continued as they struggled up the steep incline.

After clearing the hillside, Jacob led his mule down to a small patch of ground that was shaded by the hillside, rationed both some water, and gave his legs a rest. Yesterday at this hour he was rushing out of Beersheba. And with good reason, Esau's threat to kill him had so unsettled his mother that she mistreated two of their maids and purposefully knocked over the kitchen water bucket as she angrily stomped by it.

"No worries, my son," he remembered his mother's words, "you now have your father's blessing. Every relative in our family will now serve you. It was right to obtain it, even if by intrigue. *We* were right ... sometimes we must do what we must do, for your elder brother would have squandered it on careless living and would have hindered God's blessing, I know ... we were right."

And Rebekah *was* right. Esau had no thoughts of lofty endeavor, of leading a family, and keeping the altar. How many times had he embarrassed father Isaac by missing the family sacrifice because of hunting or some other reason. Too many. And Rebekah knew it well. Only *she* would ever have the courage to scold Esau, and still her reprimands always fell on deaf ears.

Esau was first born, and he knew it well. "I will do my share when my time is at hand, Mother," was his usual condescending reply. "Until then, I have a life to live in the field and in other places. One day you will understand. I am first born, and I will inherit. And when you see that, you will learn something new."

Jacob, on the other hand, had a tender heart toward his family and was always full of questions concerning the purposes of the altar. He was embarrassed with his father when Esau shirked his duties, but he always enjoyed filling in for him at the time of altar slaughter.

So Rebekah's plan was no snap decision. She had been contemplating Jacob's rightful succession for years. And yesterday, it finally had come to pass.

While Jacob relaxed in the shade of the hill, he fought off the guilt of their charade to fool his blind father. Disguising his voice and himself, even to the point of wearing an animal skin to make his skin feel hairy, was quite a deception. He knew it was right, but now, just one day after, his conscience was stinging—and Esau was fuming. Sometimes insisting on being right can really damage relationships.

But there was an excitement compelling his thoughts along this journey, too. Because Jacob was not simply fleeing Esau's wrath: he was heading to his grandfather's house to find a wife! An heir must have a heritage to pass on, and Jacob was now the heir!

"Onward, mule! Be off," he commanded, now feeling refreshed. "Three more hours and we will stop for the night."

Northward they traveled off the main road along the foot of the mountains, stopping only occasionally so Jacob could survey the distance behind to check for Esau's pursuit. The sun started to dip behind the mountains overshadowing the Great Sea, so he led his beast to a secluded spot and gathered firewood for the night.

After dinner, Jacob bedded down his mule for the night, then stared aimlessly into the fire while rehearsing the dramatic events of the past two days. Thirty minutes passed before a dry branch blew up popping sparks in his face. So he brushed himself off, untied his blanket, and used a rock near the fire for a wilderness pillow. He lay there praying for God's guidance and protection—especially from Esau.

Jacob's body was exhausted from the day's twenty-five miles, so within a few minutes he was fast asleep. Immediately, he dreamed a dream. A magnificent ladder shot down from the heavens, shaking the mountains before settling on earth. Its base glistened with a golden haze, but turned red as it disappeared upward into heaven.

Then, the rushing sound and blast of a mighty wind shook the base of the ladder as an endless troop of lightning bright figures exploded out of nowhere on both sides of the ladder in a pulsing display that illumined the night.

Angels! They were angels, ascending and descending, Jacob was made to know, because their appearances came at the speed of light. Then, their movement slowed, and Jacob could see an enormous host of robed, luminous beings, thousands upon thousands shooting up and down the ladder with the most curious expressions upon their faces. He couldn't tell if they were frowning or smiling, but he could see that their faces were the faces of men.

Then, the heavens parted, and a billowing cloud appeared above the ladder that slowly dissipated into a fine golden mist. And there, above it, stood the LORD. His eyes blazed with a penetrating fire and his presence filled the heavens. And as the rushing sounds of the angels fell silent, Jehovah spoke in Genesis 28:13 (NIV):

> *"I am the* LORD, *the God of your father Abraham and the God of Isaac. I will give you and your descendants the* **land on which you are lying,** *" His voice thundered.*
>
> *"Your descendants will be like the dust of the earth, and you will spread out to the west and to the east, to the north and to the south. All peoples on earth will be blessed through you and your offspring.*
>
> *"I am with you and will watch over you wherever you go, and I will bring you back to this land. I will not leave you until I have done what I have promised you!"*

Then the dream ended, and Jacob awakened with renewed confidence in his new day in life. *Angels ... messengers of God ... and God Himself ... I am not alone ...* were his thoughts as he arose from sleep and shook his head.

Then he looked toward the heavens in search of the ladder, raised his hands, and loudly prayed, "Surely the LORD is in this place, and I was not aware of it!"

At that moment, a solemn fear gripped Jacob's heart as he was made to realize the dream's significance and his new responsibilities as heir to Abraham's pledge.

"How awesome is this place! This is none other than the house of God; this is the gate of heaven!" he extolled in excited, new assurance.

Now he knew for sure how right he and his mother had been! God was with Him! His angels were with him. God's blessing was on him. Tomorrow he would not look over his shoulder. He would come out of hiding and travel the roads north. He actually welcomed adventures in strength and new faith! Now it was easy to lie down again to sleep through the night.

When Jacob awoke the next morning, he poured oil on the rock he had used for a pillow to make it a memorial stone. Then for the first time he vowed as Isaac's true first born heir:

"If God will be with me and will watch over me on this journey I am taking and will give me food to eat and clothes to wear so I return safely to my father's house, then the LORD will be my God and this stone that I have set up as a memorial will be God's house, and of all that you give me, I will give you a tenth."

Jacob never forgot the night that angels from heaven descended on a ladder and ministered to his troubled soul. Later in life he would wrestle with an angel before facing Esau, from whom he had manipulated a birthright. Later in life he would know the agony of being told his beloved son Joseph was dead. But in the midst of all his crises, Jacob always had a Bethel, a house of God, to remember.

His Bethel was an eternal ladder with ministering angels descending to meet his needs and ascending with his prayers to the Father's throne. The dream ceased but the ministering angels remained at his side forever. (Retold from Genesis chapters 27-28.)

Ministering Angels

It's true. God's standing order to angels is to minister to you. They don't do ministry for you. Rather, they protect, propel and prevent harm in your life so that you can do the ministry God has for you.

In spite of his mistakes and problems, Jacob discovered that on the stairway to heaven, angels were moving back and forth in ministry. You don't have to go into your future alone. God never leaves you. Jesus is with you always. The Holy Spirit indwells you. And angels are commanded to guard you, lift you up and keep you from harm.

Humble yourself. Get over your pride. Stop trying to do everything yourself. Invoke God's standing orders to allow His angels to care for you. In Hebrews we read:

> And of the angels He says, "Who makes His angels spirits and His ministers a flame of fire." (Hebrews 1:7, Amplified)

God's ministers, a flame of fire, await you to invoke God's standing orders to minister to and care for you. His fiery servants are ready to protect you, propel and lift you up and prevent harm from touching you.

Mighty Angels Waiting to be Released

Years ago I worshiped in the towering sanctuary of Trinity Church in Lubbock, Texas. During a large conference on the Holy Spirit, an altar call for salvation was given by the visiting evangelist. During that invitation, I opened my eyes which had been closed in prayer. To my amazement, two, massive warrior angels with swords drawn stood at the base of both sets of stairs leading down from the balcony to the altar area.

I asked the LORD why they stood there. "They await those who will come forward to accept Christ," the Spirit replied.

"They have been commanded by God and released by your prayers to protect the new believers from the spirits of fear and doubt as they come forward." I had been praying for God's protection from any spiritual attacks against their minds or hearts from fear, doubt or pride. In His grace, God allowed me to see the protection He had provided as He promised in Psalms 91!

In order for angels to be released and dispatched according to God's standing orders in Psalms 91, you must first be released from yourself, your sin and your past. In order to become part of God's chain of command for angels, you need to surrender your life to Jesus Christ. If you haven't done so already, pray:

> *Lord Jesus,*
> *Forgive me of my past sins and failures,*
> *I confess You as my LORD and Savior.*
> *Thank you for saving me from sin for eternal life.*
> *Thank you for the gift of your Holy Spirit.*
> *Thank you for angels encamped about me.*
> *I surrender all to you.*
> *Amen.*

As a Christian, stop ignoring resources God has given you to walk in victory, health and prosperity. Study God's Word. Give cheerfully to the work of the Kingdom of God. Be filled with the Holy Spirit. Pray always. Share the gospel with others. Serve and love others. Bear the fruit of the Holy Spirit in your life. And remember, the heavenly cohorts at your side.

So, deposit these truths in your life now:

1. God has commanded His angels concerning you.

2. God has placed you in Christ in heavenly places above the angels.

3. God has given the angels standing orders to protect you.

4. God has ordered angels to lift you up and propel you above every negative circumstance, accusing enemy or inner prison.

5. God has commanded His angels with the standing order not to allow your foot to strike a stone—no harm shall befall you.

6. So, invoke the standing orders of God to release His angels to protect, propel and prevent harm from touching you.

7. What God has commanded, you have the authority to release in the name of Jesus. What are you waiting for? Invoke the standing orders of God commanding angels concerning you!

In Seven Days, The Walls Came Down!

Deliverance!
The Angel of the LORD
encamps all around those who fear Him,
And delivers them.
—King David, (Psalms 34:7)

I want to invite you for the next seven days to pray and invoke God's standing orders for you, your family, your property, your plans and your future. Remember that the promises declared in Psalms 91 refer to the future:

- You will be delivered from the snare of the fowler and deadly pestilence (v. 3)
- You will find refuge under His wings (v. 4)
- You will not be afraid (v. 5)
- You will not be overtaken by plague or evil (v.10)

All too often when we pray, we find ourselves reacting to what has happened or is happening instead of being proactive about what's coming our way. Proactive prayer looks ahead into the future by invoking God's standing orders for angels to act on our behalf concerning what's coming. The angels can prepare the way for us so that we will be protected from any future attack of the enemy. We will be propelled over any circumstance or situation that would threaten to overcome or overwhelm us. Angels will prevent any coming weapon formed against us from prevailing.

Prayer doesn't change the past or the present; prayer shapes our future. We can go alone into future battles or we can proceed behind the hosts of the LORD. Released by our prayers, God's heavenly hosts—his armies of angels, can go ahead of us clearing the way of any hindrance, threat, harm or snare set by our enemies.

One remarkable story in Scripture outlines for us the process by which this happens. Joshua and the armies of Israel are facing a formidable obstacle—Jericho. This walled fortress of the ancient world stood between them and entering the promised land. Jericho had to be defeated. But how could a nomadic confederation of tribes comprised of the children of Egyptian slaves possibly conquer a walled fortress protected by seasoned warriors? The secret was with the captain of the LORD's army!

Reread for yourself the story of Joshua as he looks upon Jericho and ponders his future as Israel's leader:

> *And it came to pass, when Joshua was by Jericho, that he lifted his eyes and looked, and behold, a Man stood opposite him with His sword drawn in His hand. And Joshua went to Him and said to Him, "Are You for us or for our adversaries?" So He said, "No, but as Commander of the army of the LORD I have now come."*
>
> *And Joshua fell on his face to the earth and worshiped, and said to Him, "What does my Lord say to His servant?"*
>
> *Then the Commander of the LORD's army said to Joshua, "Take your sandal off your foot, for the place*

where you stand is holy." And Joshua did so.

Now Jericho was securely shut up because of the children of Israel; none went out, and none came in. And the LORD said to Joshua: "See! I have given Jericho into your hand, its king, and the mighty men of valor. You shall march around the city, all you men of war; you shall go all around the city once. This you shall do six days. And seven priests shall bear seven trumpets of rams' horns before the ark. But the seventh day you shall march around the city seven times, and the priests shall blow the trumpets.

It shall come to pass, when they make a long blast with the ram's horn, and when you hear the sound of the trumpet, that all the people shall shout with a great shout; then the wall of the city will fall down flat. And the people shall go up every man straight before him" (Joshua 5:13-6:5).

Notice these critical truths about Joshua and his impending battle:

1. The commander of the LORD's army or, as the King James translates, *the captain of the host of the LORD,* is commanding an army of angels and all the other heavenly beings.
2. The standing order for the defeat of Jericho has already been given. The LORD said to Joshua, "See! I have given Jericho into your hand ..." (6:2). The verb is *past tense.* In other words, the battle has already been decided in eternity. It's time for the angels of God to be released to implement the standing orders of God!
3. How is the release to happen? God commands Joshua's earthly army to march around the city

for six days with the seven trumpets of rams' horns before the ark. What does this represent? Spiritual warfare ... prayer ... intercession. In other words, our obedient intercession releases God's heavenly hosts to obey His standing orders.

4. On the seventh day, the day of completion, the trumpet sounds and the people lift up a great shout. What's that? Praise. God inhabits the praise of His people. Praise opens the floodgates of divine power as God's angels are released to do exactly what God wills.

5. Having done all and standing firm, the people of God witness the walls of Jericho tumbling down.

Our warfare isn't against flesh and blood, "but against principalities, against powers, against the rulers of the darkness of this age, against spiritual hosts of wickedness in the heavenly places" (Ephesians 6:12). We don't battle in the heavenly places; our prayers and praise release God's angels to do His bidding on our behalf.

I am inviting you to spend the next seven days facing your Jericho. In your path stands a walled fortress keeping you from God's destiny and promises. What must you do? It's time to pray and praise God for the victory. It's time to release the heavenly hosts to do warfare on your behalf according to His standing orders.

The next few pages define for you the spiritual, prayerful warfare that you must do daily as you march around *your* Jericho.

Pray to Invoke the Standing Orders

In the mighty name of Jesus,

I invoke the standing orders of

Almighty God

to encamp my family (or friends) [names]

with angels to protect them

in all their ways:

in their going out and coming in;

in their rising up and lying down;

in their work and in their leisure.

Amen.

Day 1

Invoking the Standing Orders

He who dwells in the secret place of the Most High
Shall abide under the shadow of the Almighty.
I will say of the LORD,
"He is my refuge and my fortress;
My God, in Him I will trust."

Surely He shall deliver you
from the snare of the fowler
And from the perilous pestilence.
He shall cover you with His feathers,
And under His wings you shall take refuge;
His truth shall be your shield and buckler.
You shall not be afraid of the terror by night,
Nor of the arrow that flies by day,
Nor of the pestilence that walks in darkness,
Nor of the destruction that lays waste at noonday.

A thousand may fall at your side,
And ten thousand at your right hand;
But it shall not come near you.
Only with your eyes shall you look,
And see the reward of the wicked.

Because you have made the LORD,
who is my refuge,
Even the Most High, your dwelling place,
No evil shall befall you,
Nor shall any plague come near your dwelling;
For He shall give His angels charge over you,
To keep you in all your ways.
In their hands they shall bear you up,
Lest you dash your foot against a stone.
—Psalms 91:1-12

Believe: God has commanded His angels to protect you, propel you over your circumstances, and prevent harm from touching you.

Declare: LORD, *You are my refuge and my fortress; My God, in You I will trust.*

Pray: LORD *Jesus, commander of the heavenly hosts, I ask you to release Your angels to protect me, my family, my property and my destiny in You. Propel me over any circumstance that would seek to flood over me. Prevent any weapon formed against me from prospering. Amen.*

Opening
Your Eyes

*Now the king of Syria was making war against Israel; and
he consulted with his servants, saying, "My camp will be in
such and such a place." And the man of God sent to the
king of Israel, saying, "Beware that you do not pass this
place, for the Syrians are coming down there."*

*Then the king of Israel sent someone to the place of which
the man of God had told him. Thus he warned him, and he
was watchful there, not just once or twice. Therefore the
heart of the king of Syria was greatly troubled by this
thing; and he called his servants and said to them,
"Will you not show me which of us is for the king of
Israel?" And one of his servants said, "None, my lord,
O king; but Elisha, the prophet who is in Israel, tells the
king of Israel the words that you speak in your bedroom."*

*So he said, "Go and see where he is, that I may send and
get him." And it was told him, saying, "Surely he is in
Dothan." Therefore he sent horses and chariots and a great
army there, and they came by night and surrounded the
city. And when the servant of the man of God arose early
and went out, there was an army, surrounding the city with*

horses and chariots. And his servant said to him,
"Alas, my master! What shall we do?"

So he answered, "Do not fear, for those who are with us are
more than those who are with them." And Elisha prayed,
and said, "Lord, I pray, open his eyes that he may see."
Then the Lord opened the eyes of the young man,
and he saw. And behold, the mountain was full of
horses and chariots of fire all around Elisha.
(2 Kings 6:8-17)

Believe: Those who are with you are more than those who are with them. 1 John 4:4 declares, "He that is in you is greater than he that is in the world."

Declare: *The Lord of hosts has surrounded me with His fiery heavenly hosts.*

Pray: *Lord of hosts, surround me, my family, my church and all those who serve and worship you with your fiery, ministering angelic hosts that we may witness your glory and victorious power. Amen.*

Day 3

Obeying His Commands

So Balaam rose in the morning, saddled his donkey,
and went with the princes of Moab. Then God's anger
was aroused because he went, and the Angel of the
LORD took His stand in the way as an adversary
against him. And he was riding on his donkey, and
his two servants were with him.

Now the donkey saw the Angel of the LORD
standing in the way with His drawn sword in His hand,
and the donkey turned aside out of the way and
went into the field. So Balaam struck the donkey to
turn her back onto the road.
(Numbers 22:21-23)

When God's angel stops you in your tracks,
learn from the donkey, not from Balaam. Decide
to obey instead of resist God. When you walk in
obedience to God's ways, His angels stand ready
to obey His standing orders on your behalf.

But if you resist God and rebel, angels obey God to block your path and seek to get your attention so that once again you will obey His commands.

———————————

Believe: Commit your way to the LORD and He will direct your paths (Psalms 37). Walk in obedience to God.

Declare: *Jesus, I love you and will obey Your voice.*

Pray: *Almighty God, as I obey your commands direct your angels to guard me in all my ways. Amen.*

Standing Firm on God's Side

Finally, my brethren, be strong in the LORD and in the power of His might. Put on the whole armor of God, that you may be able to stand against the wiles of the devil.

For we do not wrestle against flesh and blood, but against principalities, against powers, against the rulers of the darkness of this age, against spiritual hosts of wickedness in the heavenly places.

Therefore take up the whole armor of God, that you may be able to withstand in the evil day, and having done all, to stand.
(Ephesians 6:10-13)

Who is on the LORD's side? Joshua declared, ". . . as for me and my house, we will serve the LORD" (Josh. 24:15). Whose side are you on? Israel stood on God's side.

The Angel of the Lord stood between them and the armies of Egypt. Jesus warned that we cannot serve both God and mammon. We cannot straddle the fence with one foot in Egypt and the other ready to follow God.

Stop praying for God to join you. Join God in what He is doing. Seek His face. Align yourself, your family, your finances and your future with God.

———————

Believe: God's plans for you are good, not evil, to give you a hope and a future (Jeremiah 29:11-12). So determine today that you will seek and follow God's plans for your life.

Declare: *I am standing firm on God's plan for me. I will not be moved. God is my strength and refuge. His angels will keep me from stumbling.*

Pray: *Almighty God, surround me, my family and my loved ones with your angels that we will not stumble, but will stand firm against every attack of the enemy, in Jesus' name, Amen.*

Day 5

Being Set Free

Peter was therefore kept in prison, but constant
prayer was offered to God for him by the
church. And when Herod was about to bring
him out, that night Peter was sleeping, bound
with two chains between two soldiers; and the
guards before the door were keeping the prison.

Now behold, an angel of the LORD *stood by*
him, and a light shone in the prison; and he
struck Peter on the side and raised him up,
saying, "Arise quickly!" And his chains
fell off his hands.

Then the angel said to him, "Gird yourself
and tie on your sandals;" and so he did.

And he said to him, "Put on your garment
and follow me." So he went out and followed
him, and did not know that what was done
by the angel was real, but thought he was
seeing a vision.
(Acts 12:5-9)

No prison of the enemy is strong or secure enough to keep you chained and bound. God desires to liberate you from the bondage of sin and death through Jesus Christ. No emotional prison can keep you bound to guilt and failure in the past.

God's angel is coming to declare good news in your life. You have been set free!

———————

Believe: In Christ Jesus, you have nothing to hide, nothing to fear and nothing to lose. The anointing of Jesus Christ sets every captive free.

Declare: *Whenever I am bound, the truth of Jesus Christ sets me free.*

Pray: *Almighty God, thank You for setting me free from sin, guilt and bondages through the shed blood of Jesus Christ on the cross. Whenever the enemy seeks to imprison me, send forth Your angel to break the chains and open the prison doors. Amen.*

Day 6

Listening to the Good News of Angels

And suddenly there was with the angel a multitude
of the heavenly host praising God and saying:
"Glory to God in the highest,
And on earth peace, goodwill toward men!"
(Luke 2:13-14, NKJV)

Why do you focus your attention on bad news? When last did you go to others with good news instead of gossip or a bad report? Isn't it time to praise God with the angels?

Believe: God has good news for you.

Declare: *I choose to believe the good report of the* Lord.

Pray: Lord, *I join with the angels to declare praise to You and Your good news to those around me. Amen.*

Day 7

Seeing the Angel

There was a certain man in Caesarea called Cornelius,
a centurion of what was called the Italian Regiment,
a devout man and one who feared God with all his
household, who gave alms generously to the people,
and prayed to God always.
About the ninth hour of the day, he saw clearly in a
vision an angel of God coming in and saying to him,
"Cornelius!" And when he observed him, he was afraid
and said, "What is it, LORD ?" So He said to him,
"Your prayers and your alms have come up for a
memorial before God."
(Acts 10:1-4)

Start praying. Start giving. Fear God. Get prepared
for a vision from God. You can see angels!

Believe: God can open your eyes, give you a vision, and
you can see the invisible.

Declare: *God, I am believing for my entire household to*
be saved, healed and delivered.

Pray: *LORD, open my eyes so that I may see any vision*
including angels that You have for me, and live
in awe and fear of Your ways. Amen.

Other Books by Dr. Larry Keefauver

77 Irrefutable Truths of Parenting
77 Irrefutable Truths of Ministry
77 Irrefutable Truths of Marriage
77 Irrefutable Truths of Prayer
Lord, I Wish My Husband Would Pray With Me
Lord, I Wish My Teenager Would Talk With Me
Lord, I Wish My Family Would Get Saved
Hugs for Grandparents
Hugs for Heroes
When God Doesn't Heal Now
Experiencing the Holy Spirit
Praying With Smith Wigglesworth
Smith Wigglesworth on Faith
Smith Wigglesworth on Prayer
Smith Wigglesworth on Healing
Healing Words
I'm Praying for You, Friend
I'm Praying for You, Mom
Inviting God's Presence
From the Oval Office: Prayers of the Presidents

Conferences & Seminars

Growing Spiritually in Marriage
Parent-Teen Seminars
77 Irrefutable Truths About Parenting
77 Irrefutable Truths About Ministry
A Holy Spirit Encounter
The Presence-Driven Church
Commanding Angels

For Information Contact:

YourMinistryConsultationServices
Equipping the Saints (Ephesians 4:12)

Dr. Larry Keefauver
P.O. Box 2059
Sanford, FL 32772
800-750-5306 (phone) or 858-712-1986 (fax)
email: drlarry@ymcs.org
www.ymcs.org